INSPIRATIONAL STORY COLOR

MR VIVEK KUMAR PANDEY SHAMBHUNATH

ISBN 979-888569580-0

Disclaimer : Disclaimer : During Writing This Book No character & No religious , No Relation Members Are Harmed. It's Only For Study & Entertainment Purpose. Do Not Take Seriously,Written By Mr Vivek Kumar Pandey.

Contents

Contents

Foreword

In This Book There Is 30+ Inspirational Story. This Story Motivated All People With Moral Of Story. During writing this book No character & No religious are harmed written by Mr Vivek Kumar Pandey. winner youngest writer award 1st rank in india 2020.He is only one writer can publish 830+ own book that was greatest successfull in his life.This All Credit Goes To My Super Hero Daddy. This book fully colour Edition.

Preface

Author biography in English :MY NAME IS VIVEK KUMAR PANDEY . I WAS BORN IN 30 SEP 2002,I AM FROM SURAT GUJARAT INDIA.MY DREAM WAS TO BE GOOD WRITERS ,MY FAMILY SUPPORTED ME TO SUCCESSFUL AND I CAN DO IT MY SELF.How do I write? That is a question, I believe, that can be honestly answered by me."CELEBRATING YOUNGEST WRITER AWARD WINNER IN GUJARAT 1ST RANK" MR PANDEY JI . I may think I did a good job writing something . The reader is the one who decides the quality of my writing. I do find writing to be natural to me and therefore find it to be a real challenge. My trick as a challenged writer is to do the best I can and know that I am happy with the final outcome. It may take a while to do my best and there may be quite a few problems I run into along the way.

I am not a greedy person those who are thinking about me and my self I never tried it anyone people suffering from sadness ,I trying to get promoted people suffering from happiness and joy in your Life Time. Now in current situation in India and also world people are unemployed and have no many but our indian governor help to people to get free food from ration card , i also take part in leadership team ,i am Motivational speaker , Film script writer. There was my two dream firstly writer and secondly actor & also my own film is upcoming soon i done almost completely completed script for my film .I AM GOING TO SAY WORD OF HEART TOUCH OUT PLEASE READ IT" , firstly i thanks my father he supports me in this field they always getting inspired me by own his words and behavior ,they always said that he was a biggest person in the world in future and also they purchase fruit and chocolate for me in anytime & anyway , firstly my father buy him then call me Vivek you want a chocolate i will say yes papa but how many tell me ,papa: you tell me how much i buy him i told 1 or 2 chocolate but my father purchase whole the boxes of chocolate and they get suprised me. MY FATHER WAS BORN IN " 20 SEPTEMBER" 1971 IN INDIA.

1) MY FATHER FAVORITE CLOTHES IS KURTA PAIJMA AND ALSO STYLES SHOE

2) FAVORITE SINGER IS KISHORE DA

3) FAVORITE STATE GUJARAT AND KOLKATA , HIS VILLAGE IN BIHAR

4) FAVORITE COLOR BLACK AND WHITE

THEY ALSO LOVE cricket like IPL and one day t-20 .they also like watching a News daily and heard the song daily ,they also interested in tik tok video but in current time tik tok is banned in india but also few videos are in you tube. In lockdown time my family and me very enjoy day daily. my father play daily ludo with his sister and son, daughter.they always loved tea and coffee anytime call me "I . I make it tea for my father but some reason after the April to june they are suffering from fever and cough , weakness on 6 June 2020 my father death. they not told me say bye bye his life. After death of 6 June on 10 june my mom and dad anniversary.but my father is Best in the world they can do anything for me please take care of father and respect it of your parents.

CHAPTER ONE

Ch : 1 The Elephant Rope

- Ch : 1 The Elephant Rope (Belief)

Sometimes an inspiring story helps us find out the strength within us. An inspiring story helps you inspire yourself and motivate yourself. It also helps find out what you can do and what you cannot. There are hundreds you may have read in your life. But how many of them actually made changes in your mind is a question.

Here are some inspiring short stories that not only gives a powerful lesson, but can also be helpful to learn about some unknown truths about life.

A gentleman was walking through an elephant camp, and he spotted that the elephants weren't being kept in cages or held by the use of chains.

All that was holding them back from escaping the camp, was a small piece of rope tied to one of their legs.

As the man gazed upon the elephants, he was completely confused as to why the elephants didn't just use their strength to break the rope and escape the camp. They could easily have done so, but instead, they didn't try to at all.

Curious and wanting to know the answer, he asked a trainer nearby why the elephants were just standing there and never tried to escape.

The trainer replied;

"when they are very young and much smaller we use the same size rope to tie them and, at that age, it's enough to hold them. As they grow up, they are conditioned to believe they cannot break away. They believe the rope can still hold them, so they never try to break free."

The only reason that the elephants weren't breaking free and escaping from the camp was that over time they adopted the belief that it just wasn't possible.

- Moral: No matter how much the world tries to hold you back, always continue with the belief that what you want to achieve is possible. Believing you can become successful is the most important step in actually achieving it.

CHAPTER TWO

Ch : 2 Thinking Out of the Box

- Ch : 2 Thinking Out of the Box (Creative Thinking)

In a small Italian town, hundreds of years ago, a small business owner owed a large sum of money to a loan-shark. The loan-shark was a very old, unattractive looking guy that just so happened to fancy the business owner's daughter.

He decided to offer the businessman a deal that would completely wipe out the debt he owed him. However, the catch was that we would only wipe out the debt if he could marry the businessman's daughter.Needless to say, this proposal was met with a look of disgust.The loan-shark said that he would place two pebbles into a bag, one white and one black.

The daughter would then have to reach into the bag and pick out a pebble. If it was black, the debt would be wiped, but the loan-shark would then marry her. If it was white, the debt would also be wiped, but the daughter wouldn't have to marry the loan-shark.

Standing on a pebble-strewn path in the businessman's garden, the loan-shark bent over and picked up two pebbles.

Whilst he was picking them up, the daughter noticed that he'd picked up two black pebbles and placed them both into the bag.He then asked the daughter to reach into the bag and pick one.The daughter naturally had three choices as to what she could have done:

Refuse to pick a pebble from the bag.Take both pebbles out of the bag and expose the loan-shark for cheating.Pick a pebble from the bag fully well knowing it was black and sacrifice herself for her father's freedom.

She drew out a pebble from the bag, and before looking at it 'accidentally' dropped it into the midst of the other pebbles. She said to the loan-shark;

"Oh, how clumsy of me. Never mind, if you look into the bag for the one that is left, you will be able to tell which pebble I picked."

The pebble left in the bag is obviously black, and seeing as the loan-shark didn't want to be exposed, he had to play along as if the pebble the daughter dropped was white, and clear her father's debt.

- Moral: It's always possible to overcome a tough situation throughout of the box thinking, and not give in to the only options you think you have to pick from.

CHAPTER THREE

Ch : 3 The Group of Frogs

- Ch : 3 The Group of Frogs (Encouragement)

As a group of frogs was traveling through the woods, two of them fell into a deep pit. When the other frogs crowded around the pit and saw how deep it was, they told the two frogs that there was no hope left for them.

However, the two frogs decided to ignore what the others were saying and they proceeded to try and jump out of the pit.

Despite their efforts, the group of frogs at the top of the pit were still saying that they should just give up. That they would never make it out.

Eventually, one of the frogs took heed to what the others were saying and he gave up, falling down to his death. The other frog continued to jump as hard as he could. Again, the crowd of frogs yelled at him to stop the pain and just die.He jumped even harder and finally made it out. When he got out, the other frogs said, "Did you not hear us?"The frog explained to them that he was deaf. He thought they were encouraging him the entire time.

Moral: People's words can have a big effect on other's lives. Think about what you say before it comes out of your mouth. It might just be the difference between life and death.

CHAPTER FOUR

Ch : 4 A Pound of Butter

- Ch : 4 A Pound of Butter (Honesty)

There was a farmer who sold a pound of butter to a baker. One day the baker decided to weigh the butter to see if he was getting the right amount, which he wasn't. Angry about this, he took the farmer to court.

The judge asked the farmer if he was using any measure to weight the butter. The farmer replied, "Honor, I am primitive. I don't have a proper measure, but I do have a scale."The judge asked, "Then how do you weigh the butter?"

The farmer replied;

"Your Honor, long before the baker started buying butter from me, I have been buying a pound loaf of bread from him. Every day when the baker brings the bread, I put it on the scale and give him the same weight in butter. If anyone is to be blamed, it is the baker."

- Moral: In life, you get what you give. Don't try and cheat others.

CHAPTER FIVE

Ch : 5 The Obstacle In Our Path

- Ch : 5 The Obstacle In Our Path (Opportunity)

In ancient times, a King had a boulder placed on a roadway. He then hid himself and watched to see if anyone would move the boulder out of the way. Some of the king's wealthiest merchants and courtiers came by and simply walked around it.

Many people loudly blamed the King for not keeping the roads clear, but none of them did anything about getting the stone out of the way.A peasant then came along carrying a load of vegetables. Upon approaching the boulder, the peasant laid down his burden and tried to push the stone out of the road. After much pushing and straining, he finally succeeded.

After the peasant went back to pick up his vegetables, he noticed a purse lying in the road where the boulder had been.

The purse contained many gold coins and a note from the King explaining that the gold was for the person who removed the boulder from the roadway.

- Moral: Every obstacle we come across in life gives us an opportunity to improve our circumstances, and whilst the lazy complain, the others are creating opportunities through their kind hearts, generosity, and willingness to get things done.

CHAPTER SIX

Ch : 6 The Butterfly

- Ch : 6 The Butterfly (Struggles)

A man found a cocoon of a butterfly.One day a small opening appeared. He sat and watched the butterfly for several hours as it struggled to force its body through that little hole.

Until it suddenly stopped making any progress and looked like it was stuck.So the man decided to help the butterfly. He took a pair of scissors and snipped off the remaining bit of the cocoon. The butterfly then emerged easily, although it had a swollen body and small, shriveled wings.

The man didn't think anything of it and sat there waiting for the wings to enlarge to support the butterfly. But that didn't happen. The butterfly spent the rest of its life unable to fly, crawling around with tiny wings and a swollen body.

Despite the kind heart of the man, he didn't understand that the restricting cocoon and the struggle needed by the butterfly to get itself through the small opening; were God's way of forcing fluid from the body of the butterfly into its wings. To prepare itself for flying once it was out of the cocoon.

- Moral: Our struggles in life develop our strengths. Without struggles, we never grow and never get stronger, so it's important for us to tackle challenges on our own, and not be relying on help from others.

CHAPTER SEVEN

Ch : 7 Control Your Temper

- Ch : 7 Control Your Temper (Anger)

There once was a little boy who had a very bad temper. His father decided to hand him a bag of nails and said that every time the boy lost his temper, he had to hammer a nail into the fence.On the first day, the boy hammered 37 nails into that fence.

The boy gradually began to control his temper over the next few weeks, and the number of nails he was hammering into the fence slowly decreased.He discovered it was easier to control his temper than to hammer those nails into the fence.

Finally, the day came when the boy didn't lose his temper at all. He told his father the news and the father suggested that the boy should now pull out a nail every day he kept his temper under control.

The days passed and the young boy was finally able to tell his father that all the nails were gone. The father took his son by the hand and led him to the fence.

"you have done well, my son, but look at the holes in the fence. The fence will never be the same. When you say things in anger, they leave a scar just like this one. You can put a knife in a man and draw it out. It won't matter how many times you say I'm sorry, the wound is still there."

- Moral: Control your anger, and don't say things to people in the heat of the moment, that you may later regret. Some things in life, you are unable to take back.

CHAPTER EIGHT

Ch : 8 The Blind Girl

- Ch : 8 The Blind Girl (Change)

There was a blind girl who hated herself purely for the fact she was blind. The only person she didn't hate was her loving boyfriend, as he was always there for her. She said that if she could only see the world, she would marry him.

One day, someone donated a pair of eyes to her – now she could see everything, including her boyfriend. Her boyfriend asked her, "now that you can see the world, will you marry me?"

The girl was shocked when she saw that her boyfriend was blind too, and refused to marry him. Her boyfriend walked away in tears, and later wrote a letter to her saying:"Just take care of my eyes dear."

- Moral: When our circumstances change, so does our mind. Some people may not be able to see the way things were before, and might not be able to appreciate them. There are many things to take away from this story, not just one.

This is one of the inspirational short stories that left me speechless.

CHAPTER NINE

Ch : 9 Puppies for Sale

- Ch : 9 Puppies for Sale (Understanding)

A shop owner placed a sign above his door that said: "Puppies For Sale."Signs like this always have a way of attracting young children, and to no surprise, a boy saw the sign and approached the owner;

"How much are you going to sell the puppies for?" he asked.The store owner replied, "Anywhere from $30 to $50."The little boy pulled out some change from his pocket. "I have $2.37," he said. "Can I please look at them?"

The shop owner smiled and whistled. Out of the kennel came Lady, who ran down the aisle of his shop followed by five teeny, tiny balls of fur.One puppy was lagging considerably behind. Immediately the little boy singled out the lagging, limping puppy and said, "What's wrong with that little dog?"

The shop owner explained that the veterinarian had examined the little puppy and had discovered it didn't have a hip socket. It would always limp. It would always be lame.

The little boy became excited. "That is the puppy that I want to buy."

The shop owner said, "No, you don't want to buy that little dog. If you really want him, I'll just give him to you."The little boy got quite upset. He looked straight into the store owner's eyes, pointing his finger, and said;

"I don't want you to give him to me. That little dog is worth every bit as much as all the other dogs and I'll pay full price. In fact, I'll give you $2.37 now, and 50 cents a month until I have him paid for."The shop owner countered, "You really don't want to buy this little dog. He is never going to be able to run and jump and play with you like the other puppies."

To his surprise, the little boy reached down and rolled up his pant leg to reveal a badly twisted, crippled left leg supported by a big metal brace. He looked up at the shop owner and softly replied, "Well, I don't run so well myself, and the little puppy will need someone who understands!"

CHAPTER TEN

Ch : 10 Box Full of Kisses

- Ch : 10 Box Full of Kisses (Love)

Some time ago, a man punished his 3-year-old daughter for wasting a roll of gold wrapping paper. Money was tight and he became infuriated when the child tried to decorate a box to put under the Christmas tree.

Nevertheless, the little girl brought the gift to her father the next morning and said, "This is for you, Daddy."

The man became embarrassed by his overreaction earlier, but his rage continue when he saw that the box was empty. He yelled at her; "Don't you know, when you give someone a present, there is supposed to be something inside?"

The little girl looked up at him with tears in her eyes and cried;"Oh, Daddy, it's not empty at all. I blew kisses into the box. They're all for you, Daddy."

The father was crushed. He put his arms around his little girl, and he begged for her forgiveness.Only a short time later, an accident took the life of the child.

Her father kept the gold box by his bed for many years and, whenever he was discouraged, he would take out an imaginary kiss and remember the love of the child who had put it there.

- Moral: Love is the most precious gift in the world.

CHAPTER ELEVEN

Ch : 11 Baby Camel and Mother

- Ch : 11 Baby Camel and Mother

A mother and a baby camel were lying around, and suddenly the baby camel asked, "mother, may I ask you some questions? Mother said, "Sure! Why son, is there something bothering you? Baby said, "Why do camels have humps?" Mother said "Well son, we are desert animals, we need the humps to store water and we are known to survive without water". Baby said, "Okay, then why are our legs long and our feet rounded?" Mother said, "Son, obviously they are meant for walking in the desert. You know with these legs I can move around the desert better than anyone does!" Baby said, "Okay, then why are our eyelashes long? Sometimes it bothers my sight". Mother with pride said, "My son, those long thick eyelashes are your protective cover. They help to protect your eyes from the desert sand and wind".

Baby after thinking said, "I see. So the hump is to store water when we are in the desert, the legs are for walking through the desert and these eye lashes protect my eyes from the desert then what in god's name are we doing here in the Zoo!?"

- Moral: Skills, knowledge, abilities and experiences are only useful if you are at the right place.

CHAPTER TWELVE

Ch : 12 Boy's Weakness

- Ch : 12 Boy's Weakness

A 10-year-old boy decided to study judo despite the fact that he had lost his left arm in a devastating car accident.

The boy began lessons with an old Japanese judo master. The boy was doing well, so he couldn't understand why, after three months of training the master had taught him only one move. "Sensei,"(Teacher in Japanese) the boy finally said, "Shouldn't I be learning more moves?" "This is the only move you know, but this is the only move you'll ever need to know," the sensei replied.

Not quite understanding, but believing in his teacher, the boy kept training. Several months later, the sensei took the boy to his first tournament. Surprising himself, the boy easily won his first two matches. The third match proved to be more difficult, but after some time, his opponent became impatient and charged; the boy deftly used his one move to win the match. Still amazed by his success, the boy was now in the finals.

This time, his opponent was bigger, stronger, and more experienced. For a while, the boy appeared to be overmatched. Concerned that the boy might get hurt, the referee called a time-out. He was about to stop the match when the sensei intervened. "No," the sensei insisted, "Let him continue." Soon after the match resumed, his opponent made a critical mistake: he dropped his guard. Instantly, the boy used his move to pin him. The boy had won the match and the tournament.

He was the champion. On the way home, the boy and sensei reviewed every move in each and every match. Then the boy summoned the courage to ask what was really on his mind.

"Sensei, how did I win the tournament with only one move?"

"You won for two reasons," the sensei answered. "First, you've almost mastered one of the most difficult throws in all of judo. And second, the only known defense for that move is for your opponent to grab your left arm."

The boy's biggest weakness had become his biggest strength.

- Moral: Sometimes we feel that we have certain weaknesses and we blame God, the circumstances or ourselves for it but we never know that our weaknesses can become our strengths one day. Each of us is special and important, so never think you have any weakness, never think of pride or pain, just live your life to its fullest and extract the best out of it!"

CHAPTER THIRTEEN

Ch : 13 Evening Dinner with a Father

- Ch : 13 Evening Dinner with a Father

A son took his old father to a restaurant for an evening dinner. Father being very old and weak, while eating, dropped food on his shirt and trousers. Other diners watched him in disgust while his son was calm.

After he finished eating, his son who was not at all embarrassed, quietly took him to the wash room, wiped the food particles, removed the stains, combed his hair and fitted his spectacles firmly. When they came out, the entire restaurant was watching them in dead silence, not able to grasp how someone could embarrass themselves publicly like that. The son settled the bill and started walking out with his father.

At that time, an old man amongst the diners called out to the son and asked him, "Don't you think you have left something behind?".

The son replied, "No sir, I haven't".

The old man retorted, "Yes, you have! You left a lesson for every son and hope for every father".

The restaurant went silent.

- Moral: To care for those who once cared for us is one of the highest honors. We all know, how our parents cared for us for every little things. Love them, respect them, and care for them.

CHAPTER FOURTEEN

Ch : 14 Keep Your Dream

- Ch : 14 Keep Your Dream

I have a friend named Monty Roberts who owns a horse ranch in San Isidro. He has let me use his house to put on fund-raising events to raise money for youth at risk programs.

The last time I was there he introduced me by saying, "I want to tell you why I let Jack use my horse. It all goes back to a story about a young man who was the son of an itinerant horse trainer who would go from stable to stable, race track to race track, farm to farm and ranch to ranch, training horses. As a result, the boy's high school career was continually interrupted. When he was a senior, he was asked to write a paper about what he wanted to be and do when he grew up.

"That night he wrote a seven-page paper describing his goal of someday owning a horse ranch. He wrote about his dream in great detail and he even drew a diagram of a 200-acre ranch, showing the location of all the buildings, the stables and the track. Then he drew a detailed floor plan for a 4,000-square-foot house that would sit on a 200-acre dream ranch.

"He put a great deal of his heart into the project and the next day he handed it in to his teacher. Two days later he received his paper back. On the front page was a large red F with a note that read, `See me after class.‘

"The boy with the dream went to see the teacher after class and asked, `Why did I receive an F?'

"The teacher said, `This is an unrealistic dream for a young boy like you. You have no money. You come from an itinerant family. You have no resources. Owning a horse ranch requires a lot of money. You have to buy the land. You have to pay for the original breeding stock and later you'll have to pay large stud fees. There's no way you could ever do it.‘ Then the teacher added, `If you will rewrite this paper with a more realistic goal, I will reconsider your grade.'

"The boy went home and thought about it long and hard. He asked his father what he should do. His father said, `Look, son, you have to make up your own mind on this. However, I think it is a very important decision for you.' "Finally, after sitting with it for a week, the boy turned in the same paper, making no changes at all.

He stated, "You can keep the F and I'll keep my dream."

Monty then turned to the assembled group and said, "I tell you this story because you are sitting in my 4,000-square-foot house in the middle of my 200-acre horse ranch. I still have that school paper framed over the fireplace." He added, "The best part of the story is that two summers ago that same schoolteacher brought 30 kids to camp out on my ranch for a week." When the teacher was leaving, he said, "Look, Monty, I can tell you this now. When I was your teacher, I was something of a dream stealer. During those years I stole a lot of kids' dreams. Fortunately you had enough gumption not to give up on yours."

- Moral: Don't let anyone steal your dreams. Follow your heart, no matter what. No Dream is too big or too small when one works hard to live it. One should always try making dreams come true no matter what.

CHAPTER FIFTEEN

Ch : 15 Learn to Appreciate

- Ch : 15 Learn to Appreciate

Once upon a time, there was a man who was very helpful, kindhearted, and generous. He was a man who will help someone without asking anything to pay him back. He will help someone because he wants to and he loves to. One day while walking into a dusty road, this man saw a purse, so he picked it up and noticed that the purse was empty. Suddenly a woman with a policeman shows up and gets him arrested.

The woman kept on asking where did he hide her money but the man replied, "It was empty when I found it, Mam." The woman yelled at him, "Please give it back, It's for my son's school fees." The man noticed that the woman really felt sad, so he handed all his money. He could say that the woman was a single mother. The man said, "Take these, sorry for the inconvenience." The woman left and policeman held he man for further questioning.

The woman was very happy but when she counted her money later on, it was doubled, she was shocked. One day while woman was going to pay her son's school fees towards the school, she noticed that some skinny man was walking behind her. She thought that he may rob her, so she approached a policeman standing nearby. He was the same policeman, who she took along to inquire about her purse. The woman told him about the man following her, but suddenly they saw that man collapsing. They ran at him, and saw that he was the same man whom they arrested few days back for stealing a purse.

He looked very weak and woman was confused. The policeman said to the woman, "He didn't return your money, he gave you his money that day. He wasn't the thief but hearing about you son's school fees, he felt sad and gave you his money." Later, they helped man stand up, and man told the woman, "Please go ahead and pay your son's school fees, I saw you and followed you to be sure that no one steals your son's school fees." The woman was speechless.

- Moral: Life gives you strange experiences, sometime it shocks you and sometimes it may surprise you. We end up making wrong judgments or mistakes in our anger, desperation and frustration. However, when you get a second chance, correct your mistakes and return the favor. Be Kind and Generous. Learn to Appreciate what you are given.

CHAPTER SIXTEEN

Ch : 16 Learning from Mistakes

- Ch : 16 Learning from Mistakes

Thomas Edison tried two thousand different materials in search of a filament for the light bulb. When none worked satisfactorily, his assistant complained, "All our work is in vain. We have learned nothing."

Edison replied very confidently, "Oh, we have come a long way and we have learned a lot. We know that there are two thousand elements which we cannot use to make a good light bulb."

- Moral: We can also learn from our mistakes.

CHAPTER SEVENTEEN

Ch : 17 Little Boy's Meeting with God

- Ch : 17 Little Boy's Meeting with God

There once was a little boy who wanted to meet God. He knew it was a long trip to where God lived, so he packed his suitcase with Twinkies and a six-pack of root beer and started his journey. When he had gone about three blocks, he met an old woman. She was sitting in the park just staring at some pigeons.

The boy sat down next to her and opened his suitcase. He was about to take a drink from his root beer when he noticed that the old lady looked hungry, so he offered her a Twinkie. She gratefully accepted it and smiled at him. Her smile was so pretty that the boy wanted to see it again, so he offered her a root beer. Once again she smiled at him. The boy was delighted! They sat there all afternoon eating and smiling, but they never said a word.

As it grew dark, the boy realized how tired he was, and he got up to leave but before he had gone more than a few steps, he turned around, ran back to the old woman and gave her a hug. She gave him her biggest smile ever. When the boy opened the door to his own house a short time later, his mother was surprised by the look of joy on his face. She asked him, "What did you do today that made you so happy?" He replied, "I had lunch with God." But, before his mother could respond, he added, "You know what? She's got the most beautiful smile I've ever seen!"

Meanwhile, the old woman, also radiant with joy, returned to her home. Her son was stunned by the look of peace on her face and he asked, "Mother, what did you do today that made you so happy?" She replied, "I ate

Twinkies in the park with God." But, before her son responded, she added, "You know, he's much younger than I expected."

- Moral: God is everywhere. We just need to share our happiness and make others smile to feel him.

CHAPTER EIGHTEEN

Ch : 18 Smartest Man in the World

- Ch : 18 Smartest Man in the World

A doctor, a lawyer, a little boy and a priest were out for a Sunday afternoon flight on a small private plane. Suddenly, the plane developed engine trouble. In spite of the best efforts of the pilot, the plane started to go down. Finally, the pilot grabbed a parachute and yelled to the passengers that they better jump, and he himself bailed out.

Unfortunately, there were only three parachutes remaining.

The doctor grabbed one and said "I'm a doctor, I save lives, so I must live," and jumped out.

The lawyer then said, "I'm a lawyer and lawyers are the smartest people in the world. I deserve to live." He also grabbed a parachute and jumped.

The priest looked at the little boy and said, "My son, I've lived a long and full life. You are young and have your whole life ahead of you. Take the last parachute and live in peace."

The little boy handed the parachute back to the priest and said, "Not to worry Father. The smartest man in the world just took off with my back pack."

- Moral: Your job doesn't always define you, but being a Good Human being Does.

CHAPTER NINETEEN

Ch : 19 The False Human Belief

- Ch : 19 The False Human Belief

As a man was passing the elephants, he suddenly stopped, confused by the fact that these huge creatures were being held by only a small rope tied to their front leg. No chains, no cages. It was obvious that the elephants could, at anytime can break away from their bonds but for some reason, they did not.

He saw a trainer nearby and asked why these animals just stood there and made no attempt to get away. "Well," trainer said, "when they are very young and much smaller we use the same size rope to tie them and, at that age, it's enough to hold them. As they grow up, they are conditioned to believe they cannot break away. They believe the rope can still hold them, so they never try to break free."

The man was amazed. These animals could at any time break free from their bonds but because they believed they couldn't, they were stuck right where they were.

Like the elephants, how many of us go through life hanging onto a belief that we cannot do something, simply because we failed at it once before?

- Moral: Failure is a part of learning. We should never give up the struggle in life. You Fail not because you are destined to fail, but because there are lessons which you need to learn as you move on with your life.

CHAPTER TWENTY

Ch : 20 The Lion and The Mouse

- Ch : 20 The Lion and The Mouse

A Mouse running over his face awakened a Lion from sleep. Rising up angrily, he caught him and was about to kill him. Then the Mouse piteously entreated, saying:

"If you would only spare my life, I would be sure to repay your kindness." The Lion laughed at him but allowed him go. It happened shortly after this that some hunters, who bound him by strong ropes to the ground, caught the Lion. The Mouse, recognizing his roar, came and gnawed the rope with his teeth, and set him free, exclaiming:

"You ridiculed the idea of my ever being able to help you, never expecting to receive from me any repayment of your favor, Now you know that it is possible for even a Mouse to confer benefits on a Lion."

- Moral: It is possible for even a Mouse to confer benefits on a Lion.

CHAPTER TWENTY-ONE

Ch : 21 The Praying Hands

- Ch : 21 The Praying Hands

Back in the fifteenth century, in a tiny village near Nuremberg, lived a family with eighteen children. Eighteen! In order merely to keep food on the table for this mob, the father and head of the household, a goldsmith by profession, worked almost eighteen hours a day at his trade and any other paying chore he could find in the neighborhood. Despite their seemingly hopeless condition, two of Albrecht Durer the Elder's children had a dream. They both wanted to pursue their talent for art, but they knew full well that their father would never be financially able to send either of them to Nuremberg to study at the Academy.

After many long discussions at night in their crowded bed, the two boys finally worked out a pact. They would toss a coin. The loser would go down into the nearby mines and, with his earnings, support his brother while he attended the academy. Then, when that brother who won the toss completed his studies, in four years, he would support the other brother at the academy, either with sales of his artwork or, if necessary, also by laboring in the mines.

They tossed a coin on a Sunday morning after church. Albrecht Durer won the toss and went off to Nuremberg. Albert went down into the dangerous mines and, for the next four years, financed his brother, whose work at the academy was almost an immediate sensation. Albrecht's etchings, his woodcuts, and his oils were far better than those of most of his professors, and by the time he graduated, he was beginning to earn considerable fees for his commissioned works.

When the young artist returned to his village, the Durer family held a festive dinner on their lawn to celebrate Albrecht's triumphant homecoming. After a long and memorable meal, punctuated with music and laughter, Albrecht rose from his honored position at the head of the table to drink a toast to his beloved brother for the years of sacrifice that had enabled Albrecht to fulfill his ambition. His closing words were, "And now, Albert, blessed brother of mine, now it is your turn. Now you can go to Nuremberg to pursue your dream, and I will take care of you."

All heads turned in eager expectation to the far end of the table where Albert sat, tears streaming down his pale face, shaking his lowered head from side to side while he sobbed and repeated, over and over, "No ...no ...no ...no."

Finally, Albert rose and wiped the tears from his cheeks. He glanced down the long table at the faces he loved, and then, holding his hands close to his right cheek, he said softly, "No, brother. I cannot go to Nuremberg. It is too late for me. Look ... look what four years in the mines have done to my hands! The bones in every finger have been smashed at least once, and lately I have been suffering from arthritis so badly in my right hand that I cannot even hold a glass to return your toast, much less make delicate lines on parchment or canvas with a pen or a brush. No, brother ... for me it is too late."

More than 450 years have passed. By now, Albrecht Durer's hundreds of masterful portraits, pen and silver-point sketches, watercolors, charcoals, woodcuts, and copper engravings hang in every great museum in the world, but the odds are great that you, like most people, are familiar with only one of Albrecht Durer's works. More than merely being familiar with it, you very well may have a reproduction hanging in your home or office.

One day, to pay homage to Albert for all that he had sacrificed, Albrecht Durer painstakingly drew his brother's abused hands with palms together and thin fingers stretched skyward. He called his powerful drawing simply "Hands," but the entire world almost immediately opened their hearts to his great masterpiece and renamed his tribute of love "The Praying Hands."

- Moral: The next time you see a copy of that touching creation, take a second look. Let it be your reminder, if you still need one, that no one - no one - ever makes it alone!

CHAPTER TWENTY-TWO

Ch : 22 The White Elephant

- Ch : 22 The White Elephant

Once upon a time, there lived a herd of eighty thousand elephants at the bottom of the majestic Himalayas. Their leader was a magnificent and rare white elephant who was an extremely kind-hearten soul. He greatly loved his mother who had grown blind and feeble and could not look out for herself.

Each day this white elephant would go deep into the forest in search of food. He would look for the best of wild fruit to send to his mother. But alas, his mother never received any. This was because his messengers would always eat them up themselves. Each night, when he returned home he would be surprised to hear that his mother had been starving all day. He was absolutely disgusted with his herd.

Then one day, he decided to leave them all behind and disappeared in the middle of the night along with his dear mother. He took her to Mount Candorana to live in a cave beside a beautiful lake that was covered by gorgeous pink lotuses.

It so happened that one day, when the white elephant was feeding he heard loud cries. A forester from Benaras had lost his way in the forest and was absolutely terrified. He had come to the area to visit relatives and could not find his way out.

On seeing this big white elephant he was even more terrified and ran as fast as he could. The elephant followed him and told him not to be afraid, as all he wanted to do was to help him. He asked the forester why he was crying so bitterly. The forester replied that he was crying because he had been roaming the forest for the past seven days and could not find his way out.

The elephant told him not to worry as he knew every inch of this forest and could take him to safety. He then lifted him on to his back and carried him to the edge of the forest from where the forester went on his merry way back to Benaras.

On reaching the city, he heard that King Brahmadutta's personal elephant had just died and the King was looking for a new elephant. His heralds were roaming the city, announcing that any man who had seen or heard of an elephant fit for a King should come forward with the information.

The forester was very excited and immediately went up to the King and told him about the white elephant that he had seen on Mount Candorana. He told him that he had marked the way and would require the help of the elephant trainers in order to catch this fantastic elephant.

The King was quite pleased with the information and immediately dispatched a number of soldiers and elephant trainers along with the forester. After travelling for many days, the group reached the lake besides which the elephants resided. They slowly moved down to the edge of the lake and hid behind the bushes. The white elephant was collecting lotus shoots for his mother's meal and could sense the presence of humans. When he looked up, he spotted the forester and realized that it was he who had led the King's men to him. He was very upset at the ingratitude but decided that if he put up a struggle many of the men would be killed. And he was just too kind to hurt anyone. So he decided to go along with them to Benaras and then request the benevolent King to be set free.

That night when the white elephant did not return home, his mother was very worried. She had heard all the commotion outside and had guessed that the King's men had taken away her son. She was scared that the King would ride him in to battle and her son would definitely be killed. She was also worried that there would be no one to look after her or even feed her, as she could not see. She just lay down and cried bitterly.

Meanwhile her son was led in to the beautiful city of Benaras where he was given a grand reception. The whole city was decorated and his own stable was gaily painted and covered with garlands of fragrant flowers. The trainers laid out a feast for their new state elephant who refused to touch a morsel. He did not respond to any kind of stimuli, be it the fragrant flowers or the beautiful and comfortable stable. He just sat there looking completely despondent.

The worried trainers went straight to report the situation to their King, as they were scared that the elephant would just waste away without any food or water. The King was extremely concerned when he heard what they had to say and went to the stable himself. He offered the elephant food from the royal table and asked him why he grieved in this manner. He thought that the elephant should be proud and honored that he was chosen as the state elephant and would get the opportunity to serve his King.

But the white elephant replied that he would not eat a thing until he met his mother. So the King asked him where his mother was. The elephant replied that she was back home on Mount Candorana and must be worried and hungry as she was blind and had no one to feed her and take care of her. He was afraid that she would die.

The compassionate King was touched by the elephant's story and asked him to return to his blind, old mother and take care of her as he had been doing all along. He set him free in love and kindness. The happy elephant went running home as fast as he could. And he was relieved to find that his mother was still alive. He filled his trunk with water and poured it over his sick mother who thought that it was raining. Then she cried out as she thought that some evil spirit had come to harm her and wished and prayed that her son was there to save her.

The white elephant gently bent over his blind mother and stroked her lovingly. She immediately recognized his touch and was overjoyed. Her son lifted her up and told her that the kind and compassionate King of Benaras had set him free and he was here to love and look after his mother forever.

His mother was absolutely thrilled and blessed the kind King with peace, prosperity and joy till the end of his days. She was so thankful to him for sending her son back home. The white elephant was able to take good care of his mother till the day she died. And when he died himself, the King erected a statue of him by the side of the lake and held an annual elephant festival there in memory of such a caring and noble soul.

- Moral: Always give affection and care to our dear ones. Always respect other's feelings.

CHAPTER TWENTY-THREE

Ch : 23 Old Witch and Noble Knight

- Ch : 23 Old Witch and Noble Knight

Once there was a very noble name Arthur who was captured by his neighboring king. Enemy could have killed him but Enemy king knew that he was very wise and noble king. So he offered him freedom but on one condition.

He would have to figure out an answer and even if after an year Arthur wouldn't be able to answer then he would be put to death.

Question was : What does a woman really wants??

Even most knowledgeable wouldn't be able to answer that but still Arthur accepted Enemy king preposition as it was better than death.

Arthur returned to his kingdom and begin to ask everyone about it but no one was able to give any satisfactory answer.

Many people advised him to consult an old witch but she was famous for charging exorbitant prices. For whole year Arthur avoided going to witch but last day came and he had no other option but to go to witch.

He went to her and told him about his problem. Witch agreed to help him but for a price in return. Price was : Witch wanted to marry Gwen.. most noble night and Arthur's closet friend.

Arthur was horrified to know price as witch was very ugly looking hideous and smelled very bad. Arthur didn't wanted to force his friend to marry such repugnant creature so he refused.

Later Gwen got to know about witch proposal and talked to Arthur. Same night Gwen and witch wedding was proclaimed and Witch answered Arthur question..

Answer was : What woman really want is to be in charge of her own life.

Arthur went back to neighboring kingdom and Enemy king was satisfied by answer and hence granted Arthur his freedom. Even after getting his freedom back Arthur was not happy because for this his best friend Gwen had to marry an old Witch.

Next day, honeymoon hour approached. Gwen prepared his mind for worst but to his surprise inside room was awaiting the most beautiful woman he had ever seen.

Witch said to Gwen, "I would be horrible and ugly witch half the time and beautiful maiden self for half.. Which would you want me to be during the day and which during the night??

Would you prefer a beautiful maiden during to show off to your friends but at night an old witch.. or would you prefer an old hideous witch during day but by night a beautiful women to be with??".

Gwen replied, "I would like you to choose that for yourself.."

Hearing this witch announced that she would be beautiful all the time because he had respected her enough to be in-charge of her life..

- Moral: Treat Woman with Respect and let her be the One to decide for Herself.

CHAPTER TWENTY-FOUR

Ch : 24 Young Man in the Plane

- Ch : 24 Young Man in the Plane

Once a Sikh young man was traveling in first class of an airline. After flight took off, air hostess came to him and offered him complimentary drinks as per airlines guidelines.

Air hostess bought an alcohol drink, young man refused for that drink. Air hostess returned with that drink to her kitchen. After sometime she came back with another alcohol drink better looking than drink she had before.

Young man declined politely again for the drink. Air hostess felt surprised and bit troubled by this.

Air hostess took it to pride and wasn't able to accept no for service and drink offered to young man. So, Just after a while she came back with more decorated drink and presented it to young man but again young man refused.

Air hostess asked, "Sir, you feel a lack of service in the bid that due to which you are not drinking? This is complimentary.."

Young man replied, "I am follower of Satguru and i don't drink alcoholic drinks."

Air hostess still insisted him to take drink.

Young man replied, "Ok, if you insist so much i will drink but only on one condition, first ask your pilot to have this drink.. only then i will accept.."

Air hostess looked at him and with hesitation replied, "But sir he is on duty and if he drinks it then there is chance of plane crash.."

Young man smiled and replied, "As you pilot can't drink on duty.. similarly is with me.. I am always on duty and my duty is that I have to adhere to the words of my guru, as if your pilot is to save the plane in every situation, in the same way I have to save my faith."

Air hostess felt ashamed for her behavior and apologized.

CHAPTER TWENTY-FIVE

Ch : 25 Whose Prayers were Answered?

- Ch : 25 Whose Prayers were Answered?

Once a ship was wrecked at sea due to storm and only out of all crew two men were bale to swim themselves to a small deserted island.

After both reached island, they didn't know what to do and both talked and they reached on conclusion that there is nothing they can do except to pray to God and wait for rescue.

However, they both decided to divide territory between both of them and stay at opposite side of it. They did this to determine whose prayers would be more effective.First thing they needed was food. So first man prayed for food and next day he saw fruits bearing trees on his side and saw that other man's side was still barren.

After two weeks, first man felt lonely and prayed for wife and next day a women survivor from ship wreck swam to his side of land. On other side there was still nothing.

Next first man prayed for home and clothes and more food. Like magic he got all those things. Still other man side was same as before nothing changed.

Finally first man prayed for ship so that he and his wife could leave that island. Next morning a Ship docked at his side of island.

He boarded on ship with his wife. Then first man thought, "Since none of that person prayers have been answered. He is unworthy of leaving that island." First man decided to leave other man on island.

As ship was about to leave, first man heard a voice from sky saying, "Why are you leaving your companion on island??"

First man replied, "Since i got everything i prayed for That means my blessings are result of my faith and prayers. His prayers were unanswered that why he has nothing on his side and so i figured he does not deserve to leave island with me."

Voice from sky responded, "You are sorely mistaken. You are in great debt to that man."

"How is that?", asked first man.

"It was that person's faith and prayer that invoked your blessings as he was one who prayed that all your prayers might be answered." replied voice from sky.

• Moral:

Never Judge Other's on what you See.

CHAPTER TWENTY-SIX

Ch : 26 Way to Achieve Goal

- Ch : 26 Way to Achieve Goal

One day master was watching a practice session in courtyard. All students were doing their practices.

Among all those students he noticed that there was one young man who was trying to perfect his technique but he is not able to work on that move properly and it seemed to master that young man was getting disturbed by the presence of other students.

Master could sense that young man's frustration and went up to young man and tapped on his shoulder.

He questioned to young man, "What's bothering you?"

Young man replied with strained expression, "I don't know..I don't understand why i am not able to execute this move properly. No matter how much i try.."

Master replied, "Listen, before you can master technique, you should understand Harmony. Come with me, i will explain you how you can do that?"

Master and student left building and walked some distance into forest until they reach a stream. After reaching there master and student stood silently on the bank of stream for sometime.

After a while master spoke to young man pointing at the stream, "Look at the stream. See there are rocks in its way, does it slam them out of frustration??"

No.. It will not slam those rocks but instead stream will simply flow around them and move on.. Be like water and you will know what Harmony is.."

Young man understood master's advise and went back to courtyard to practice his move and this time, he concentrated his focus on move and barely notice other students around him and then he was able to executed the perfect move and master that technique .

- Moral:

If we want To Achieve our Goal then we must try to get in Harmony with ourselves and not Let presence of Other people bother Us.

CHAPTER TWENTY-SEVEN

Ch : 27 The Window Story for Inspiration

- Ch : 27 The Window Story for Inspiration

It's story of two men who were both seriously ill and occupied same room at hospital.One man was next to room's only window and allowed to get only for one hour to sit up during his treatment of lungs. Other man had to spend all day lying flat on his back.

Both men talked for hours. They spoke about their wives, families, home, job, vacation. Every afternoon when men next to room window would sit, he would pass time by describing scenery outside window to his roommate.

The man in the other bed would love that one hour periods where his world would be broaden and activities and colors of outside world. As the man by the window described all the exquisite details of outside world and other man would close his eyes and imagine those scene.

One afternoon man by the window described a very beautiful parade passing by the window. In-spite other man couldn't hear the band but he could imagine all the things man by window described him. Suddenly a thought crossed his mind, " Why should he have all the pleasure of seeing everything and i get to see nothing."

As days passed guy started to miss seeing sights more and more. His envy got over him and soon turned him sour. He was unable to sleep and thought now should control his life.

Late one night as he was lying looking at the ceiling, the man by window started coughing. He was chocking on his fluids and other man watched in dim light of room. As struggling man by window trying to get hold for button to call for help. Even listening this other man never moved, never pushed his own button which would have bought nurse running. In less than five minutes man by window chocking stopped along with sound of breathing. Now there was only deathly silence.

Next morning nurse arrived to bring water for both of them. She saw there lifeless body of man by window. As soon as man found it appropriate he asked if he could move to bed next to window. The nurse made the switch and after making sure he was comfortable, She left him alone.

After moving to bed next to window, slowly painfully he tried to get up to take his first look out side the window. He was excited that he would finally get to see outside window. He slowly turn to look out the window beside the bed and to his surprise window was facing " Blank Wall " .

- Moral:

It's our choice to keep Positive Attitude towards Life. Circumstances are just parts of what makes us Joyful. Pursuit of Happiness is an Inward Journey. If we continue to bit our lips and just before we begin to complain we should shoot that seemingly harmless negative thought as it germinates, We will find there is much Rejoice about.

CHAPTER TWENTY-EIGHT

Ch : 28 Three Feet From Gold

- Ch : 28 Three Feet From Gold

During the gold rush, a man who had been mining in Colorado for several months quit his job, as he hadn't struck gold yet and the work was becoming tiresome. He sold his equipment to another man who resumed mining where it had been left off. The new miner was advised by his engineer that there was gold only three feet away from where the first miner stopped digging.

The engineer was right, which means the first miner was a mere three feet away from striking gold before he quit.

- Moral:

When things start to get hard, try to persevere through the adversity. Many people give up on following their dreams because the work becomes too difficult, tedious, or tiresome—but often, you're closer to the finish line than you may think, and if you push just a little harder, you will succeed.

CHAPTER TWENTY-NINE

Ch : 29 Rocks, Pebbles, and Sand

- Ch : 29 Rocks, Pebbles, and Sand

A philosophy professor once stood up before his class with a large empty mayonnaise jar. He filled the jar to the top with large rocks and asked his students if the jar was full.

His students all agreed the jar was full. He then added small pebbles to the jar, and gave the jar a bit of a shake so the pebbles could disperse themselves among the larger rocks. Then he asked again, "Is the jar full now?"

The students agreed that the jar was still full.

The professor then poured sand into the jar to fill up all the remaining empty space.

The students then agreed again that the jar was full.

The Metaphor:

In this story, the jar represents your life and the rocks, pebbles, and sand are the things that fill up your life. The rocks represent the most important projects and things you have going on, such as spending time with your family and maintaining proper health. This means that if the pebbles and the sand were lost, the jar would still be full and your life would still have meaning.

The pebbles represent the things in your life that matter, but that you could live without. The pebbles are certainly things that give your life meaning (such as your job, house, hobbies, and friendships), but they are not critical for you to have a meaningful life. These things often come and go, and are not permanent or essential to your overall well-being.

Finally, the sand represents the remaining filler things in your life, and material possessions. This could be small things such as watching television, browsing through your favorite social media site, or running errands. These things don't mean much to your life as a whole, and are likely only done to waste time or get small tasks accomplished.

- The Moral:

The metaphor here is that if you start with putting sand into the jar, you will not have room for rocks or pebbles. This holds true with the things you let into your life. If you spend all of your time on the small and insignificant things, you will run out of room for the things that are actually important.

In order to have a more effective and efficient life, pay attention to the "rocks," because they are critical to your long-term well-being.

CHAPTER THIRTY

Ch : 30 A Wise Man's Jokes

- Ch : 30 A Wise Man's Jokes

A wise man once faced a group of people who were complaining about the same issues over and over again. One day, instead of listening to the complaints, he told them a joke and everyone cracked up laughing.

Then, the man repeated the joke. A few people smiled.Finally, the man repeated the joke a third time–but no one reacted.The man smiled and said, "You won't laugh at the same joke more than once. So what are you getting from continuing to complain about the same problem?"

- Moral:

You're not going to get anywhere if you keep complaining about the same problem but do nothing to fix it. Don't waste your time complaining, expecting other people to continue to react to your complaints. Instead, take action to make a change.

CHAPTER THIRTY-ONE

Ch : 31 It's Never Too Late

- Ch : 31 It's Never Too Late

In the 1940s, there was a man who, at the age of 65, was living off of $99 social security checks in a small house, driving a beat-up car.He decided it was time to make a change, so he thought about what he had to offer that other people may benefit from. His mind went to his fried chicken recipe, which his friends and family loved.

He left his home state of Kentucky and traveled throughout the country, trying to sell his recipe to restaurants. He even offered the recipe for free, asking for only a small chunk of the money that was earned.

However, most of the restaurants declined his offer. In fact, 1,009 restaurants said no.

But even after all of the rejections, he persisted. He believed in himself and his chicken recipe.

When he visited restaurant #1,010, he got a YES.

His name? Colonel Hartland Sanders.

- Moral:

There are a few lessons that you can take away from this story. First, it's never too late in life to find success. In a society that often celebrates young, successful people, it's easy to start to think you're never going to be successful after a certain age. However, Colonel Sanders is an example that proves that argument wrong.

This story also demonstrates the power of persistence. You have to have confidence in yourself and believe in your work for other people to believe it also. Disregard anyone who tells you "no" and simply move on.

Thank You So Much Message

For Your Supported & For Your Loves Thank You So Much. Have A Greatest Day Of Your. If I am successful today, because of my father, if he lived today, he would have been very happy, he will always and always be with me.